Preface

The Economic Issues series was inaugurated in September 1996. Its aim is to make accessible to a broad readership of nonspecialists some of the economic research being produced in the International Monetary Fund on topical issues. The raw material of the series is drawn mainly from IMF Working Papers, technical papers produced by Fund staff members and visiting scholars, as well as from policy-related research papers. This material is refined for the general readership by editing and partial redrafting.

The following paper draws on material originally contained in IMF Working Paper 95/146, "Transformation of Markets and Policy Instruments for Open Market Operations" by Stephen H. Axilrod, who was a consultant with the Fund in 1995. Neil Wilson collaborated in the preparation of the present version. Readers interested in the original Working Paper may purchase a copy from IMF Publication Services.

ECONOMIC ISSUES 5

Transformations to Open Market Operations

Developing Economies and Emerging Markets

Stephen H. Axilrod

INTERNATIONAL MONETARY FUND
WASHINGTON, D.C.

ISBN: 1-55775-627-9

ISSN: 1020-5098

Published December 1996

Reprinted May 1997

To order IMF publications, please contact:

International Monetary Fund, Publication Services
700 19th Street, N.W., Washington, D.C. 20431, U.S.A.
Tel.: (202) 623-7430 Telefax: (202) 623-7201
Internet: publications@imf.org

Transformations to Open Market Operations: Developing Economies and Emerging Markets

By buying or selling bonds, bills, and other financial instruments in the open market, a central bank can expand or contract the amount of reserves in the banking system and can ultimately influence the country's money supply. When the central bank sells such instruments it absorbs money from the system. Conversely, when it buys it injects money into the system. This method of trading in the market to control the money supply is called open market operations.

Open market operations are the major instrument of monetary control in industrial countries and are becoming important to developing countries and economies in transition. Open market operations allow central banks great flexibility in the timing and volume of monetary operations at their own initiative, encourage an impersonal, businesslike relationship with participants in the marketplace, and provide a means of avoiding the inefficiencies of direct controls. Developing indirect controls is important to the process of economic development because, as a country's markets expand, direct controls tend to become less effective, and markets eventually find a way around them, especially in a global world economy. With more countries seeking to deregulate and unleash the potential of market forces, many policymakers and central bankers are grappling with ways to realize the full benefits of open market operations.

For such operations to become part of monetary policy, however, other monetary instruments now in place need to be adjusted and the market infrastructure must be transformed. This paper assesses the options available to a central bank for addressing these matters and designing instruments for implementing open market operations. First, it provides a brief review of the connection between open market operations and other monetary operations. Then, it discusses how the central bank can encourage development of the necessary financial market architecture. Finally, it reviews the advantages and limitations of specific approaches to open market operations.

How Are Open Market Operations Related to Other Monetary Instruments?

Open market operations affect the money supply and related financial measures through their impact on the reserve base of the banking system. As a matter of monetary policy tactics in controlling these reserves, open market operations can be conducted in one of two ways: actively, by aiming for a given quantity of reserves and allowing the price of reserves (that is, the interest rate) to fluctuate freely; or passively, by aiming at a particular interest rate, allowing the amount of reserves to fluctuate. Industrial countries, with well-developed and sensitive markets, normally employ a passive approach, although there have been exceptions. A passive approach also appears to be the norm in emerging markets that have reached a certain level of sophistication. There are advantages to a more active approach in developing countries, however. In such countries, the absence of efficient secondary or interbank markets—to transmit the influence of monetary policy—might be one reason for an active approach. Another might be that the active approach allows the central bank to define its policies more clearly, especially when control of inflation is the overriding goal. Such an approach is embodied in a number of programs supported by the International Monetary Fund for particular countries.

If open market operations are to become the principal policy instrument, other monetary instruments obviously need to be given less importance, particularly the central bank's discount window, where the banking system can obtain reserves on its own initiative simply by borrowing from the central bank. Other adjustments may also be needed, depending in part on the particular strategy adopted for conducting day-to-day open market operations.

Discount Window Policy

For open market operations to be effective, limitations need to be placed on the access of banks to borrowing from the central bank at the discount window. Without such limitations, open market operations could not be used as the principal monetary instrument for controlling bank reserves and overall financial conditions. The discount window should therefore be designed to make access to the central bank's credit less attractive in one way or another, perhaps through a high penalty rate or restrictive guidelines. Some countries, such as Germany, employ a dual rate structure, comprising a basic discount rate and a penalty Lombard rate, to discourage overuse of this facility.

Restrictions on the discount window need, however, to be handled with care. If a penalty rate is set well above current market conditions, the system might not react quickly enough to unanticipated liquidity demands. Guidelines that restrict access to the window ought to permit smooth adjustment when reserve shortages occur. In a tight money period, borrowing from the central bank for very limited periods allows banks to make more orderly portfolio adjustments. Such short-term borrowing at the discount window should be differentiated from longer-term structural borrowing at the window, which, among other things, allows emergency long-term advances to institutions in severe operating difficulties.

Reserve Requirements

In addition to use of the discount window, imposing reserve requirements has traditionally been used by central banks as a means of monetary control. The ability to vary the proportion of assets that banks are required to hold in reserve is an obvious means of controlling the money supply. Reserve requirements can be regarded as either an alternative to open market operations or a way of enhancing their effectiveness for monetary control purposes. Since the use of open market operations has become more widespread, central banks have, in fact, had less recourse to changes in reserve requirements, which are a relatively crude tool. In many countries, they have also gradually been lowered and, in some cases, eliminated, since such requirements can place banks at a significant competitive disadvantage to other institutions providing similar services.

A minimum binding level of reserve requirements may be useful in helping to gauge the impact of open market operations on interest rates and the money supply. The experience of some countries that do not impose reserve ratios, such as the United Kingdom, may suggest that they are not really necessary. On the other hand, the financial crisis at the end of 1994 in Mexico, which had abolished reserve requirements, raises questions about whether such requirements—and the ability to vary them—could still play a useful role. They may be particularly useful in circumstances where bank liquidity needs to be adjusted rapidly in markets that are thin, and where the central bank needs to give clear, swift, and unambiguous signals on the need for expansion or contraction of the money supply. Even in the United States, with its highly developed money market, reserve requirements remain binding on transaction deposits. The ability to make relatively predictable estimates of required reserves seems to be particularly useful to the Federal Reserve in its decisions on the timing and size of open market operations.

The Market and the Role of the Central Bank

As an economy grows, financial markets can be expected to broaden and deepen, but experience shows that the pace and pattern of market development may need guidance from monetary and government authorities. The associated development of open market policy instruments tends to occur in two stages. First, there is a shift away from direct controls toward use of open market operations in the primary market through auctions of new issues of securities. Later, there will be a further shift toward the use of fully flexible two-way operations in existing securities as active secondary markets develop. In addition to their policy function, open market operations in primary markets can be viewed as a prelude to—and helpful in—the evolution of active secondary markets.

Suitability of Markets

Ideal conditions for flexible open market operations exist in few developing or transition economies. Nevertheless, open market operations of one sort or another can and should be undertaken in markets that may not be entirely ideal but are at varying stages of development toward a deregulated, competitive system. In such cases, operations may need to be limited in size or employed only periodically. The participation of the central bank should hasten market development, though the bankdoes need to take care that this does not compromise or add to the riskiness of its own balance sheet, which may in turn diminish its credibility and stature. A central bank will be able to function more effectively if markets perceive that its portfolio of assets is highly liquid and essentially risk free.

The markets most suitable for flexible open market operations are normally those where short-term instruments are traded, though it should be possible—and may sometimes be desirable—to trade in instruments with various maturities. Well-developed markets are characterized by a large and continuous volume of trading by a variety of participants, including government, financial institutions, and other businesses.

Three sectors present the best opportunities for effective open market operations. These are the markets for government and central bank securities, for interbank debt, and for short-term instruments issued by financial institutions and other corporate entities, including commercial paper, finance company paper, and bank certificates of deposit.

Given the government's ability to raise taxes, the government securities market is generally regarded to be free of credit risk and therefore the best medium for open market operations. Unstable political and economic conditions, however, may make it impossible to maintain a viable market for issuing debt. Political stability and a sustained government record of meeting interest payments and redemption schedules are therefore essential to the use of open market operations. Apart from a failure to meet such contractual obligations, a government securities market can also dry up if the central bank pursues an inflationary policy that drives investors out of the market by eroding the real value of outstanding debt. Thus, keeping inflation within acceptable bounds is also a vital precondition.

Short-term private debt, including interbank debt, is less suitable for open market operations not only because of its inherent credit risks but because it leaves the central bank with some awkward choices. If the central bank is willing to buy this debt, commercial concerns may take the opportunity to off-load riskier paper. And if the central bank suddenly refuses, the market may turn away from such paper entirely, possibly precipitating a crisis. One way to resolve this type of quandary is for the central bank to restrict its operations to paper that carries a suitable credit rating, as established by an independent rating agency. In circumstances in which the amount of government debt is low or fast declining, central banks can find that open market operations are necessarily restricted to private money market instruments. When this occurs, operations in commercial bank instruments or interbank debt may raise fewer difficult credit risk issues than in other private instruments given the ongoing relationships between banks and the central bank. If a significant government debt market does not exist, a central bank may decide to create a similar balance sheet effect by developing debt instruments of its own, or through the use of a special government issue employed only for monetary policy purposes. These could serve as a permanent and liquid addition to the central bank balance sheet, substituting for private assets.

Regulatory Role of the Central Bank

Both the central bank and the government need a reliable marketplace for government securities, where participants feel secure that counterparties will perform according to their obligations and which is transparent enough to encourage wide participation. To obtain its objectives through open market operations the central bank should establish performance standards for participants. This is also the natural focal point for market surveillance through gathering statistics and publishing market aggregates.

The central bank may not wish to go beyond these functions by assuming direct regulatory and oversight responsibilities, which may unduly tax its limited personnel resources and expose the central bank to a loss of stature and credibility should scandals erupt in the government securities market—as they sometimes do. A division of labor between monetary policy operations (the responsibility of the central bank) and regulatory authority (the responsibility of some other agency or, if within the central bank, of a department separate from open market operations) may serve a nation's interest better. This said, the public will tend to look to the central bank as bearing some responsibility for markets in which it operates, whatever its precise role. For this reason alone, the central bank's market group should take steps that help rationalize the market's architecture and enhance its performance.

Market Architecture

A central bank generally prefers to operate in a transparent market that trades continuously, where communication of its operations is prompt, and in which its purposes are well understood. It can take steps to help achieve these goals, such as promoting an interbank market, designing market instruments and trading infrastructure, providing financing facilities, establishing criteria for dealing with the central bank's open market function, collecting and disseminating statistics, and encouraging a safe payments and clearing mechanism.

An active interbank market is particularly important because it helps clarify the timing and volume of open market operations. Many countries have developed such a market by adjusting policy instruments. The more successful have also used discount window policies that discourage, penalize, or forbid short-term borrowing at the central bank. The central bank can also encourage interbank trading through more technical measures, such as using its transfer and settlement mechanism to assure the integrity of interbank flows.

The central bank should take the lead, along with the Treasury, in encouraging market practices conducive to competitive trading. It could, for instance, encourage a computerized system of bids and offers for securities that protects anonymity. To foster market transparency, it should also discourage trading from taking place outside the established markets. The Treasury should have equal or greater interest in competitive trading, given that the cost of national debt should fall as government securities become more liquid.

Prior to the emergence of an active interbank and money market, the availability of an official financing facility can be particularly helpful at the early stages of market development. It can encourage market-makers to take positions and carry an adequate inventory, a necessary condition for a liquid market.

Many countries have been moving toward use of repurchase agreements (repos) as the most flexible and convenient form of financing. Repos, by which market participants buy or sell securities in return for cash with an agreement to reverse the transaction at a later point, are seen as an effective instrument for increasing market liquidity and helping to smooth the way to broader market development. They are usually short term, but may have longer maturities.

The central bank should make it clear that the availability of such financing depends primarily on monetary policy rather than strictly market considerations. Nonetheless, it may give a little more consideration to market needs at early stages of development. It may consider, for instance, whether a relatively favorable financing rate should be offered to encourage the emergence of active market-makers. In doing so, however, it should also take into account the political problems that often accompany subsidies and the inconsistency of treating some market participants favorably when it is trying to encourage competition. Indeed, in most cases, official financing should be provided at a competitive rather than favorable rate, even for a transitional period.

The central bank can also encourage market development by setting down ground rules for parties with which it deals. Criteria for a business relationship with the central bank may include membership in a group of primary dealers. A number of countries conduct open market operations through such primary dealers, who have an obligation to make reasonable bids and offers when the central bank enters the market, as well as in Treasury auctions. Brazil, the Czech Republic, India, Malaysia, the Philippines, Poland, and Russia, for example, have all introduced, or are introducing, such primary dealer systems. To perform their function more effectively, dealers would also have to seek retail customers, and would thereby help develop a broader and more liquid market.

In smaller countries, the creation of a primary dealer system where the number of participants may be few may be more problematic and impractical. When a market becomes large enough, however, there is much to be said for confining operations to a group of dealers, perhaps by designating a minimum level of capital. In order to avoid charges of favoritism, the group may have to be quite large. But, by establishing such a group, the central bank will be in a stronger position to encourage dealers to establish better market-making standards, such as minimum transaction sizes for dealing at quoted prices. Of course, ongoing rapid technological changes will also influence the best approach for the central bank to take toward market structure and its own counterparties.

The central bank is the natural focus for collection and dissemination of market statistics. The process of data collection, including daily figures on positions, transactions volume, and financing by type of issue, should begin at the very earliest stages of development. These figures provide the basis for surveillance. Later, when the number of participants is sufficient so that individual firm data cannot be deduced, the central bank should be able to publish aggregate data on market activity, something it should do as quickly as possible in order to enhance market transparency. Publication should be timed with sufficient lag, perhaps a week or a month, depending on the instrument, to avoid market overreaction.

The central bank should also take the lead at an early stage in encouraging the market to set delivery and payment standards. No market functions effectively without reasonable assurance that securities will be delivered on time and paid for as agreed. Although the speed and reliability of the clearing and payments systems obviously depend on the market's technical capacity and institutional arrangements, the central bank can play a powerful role in galvanizing such efforts because of its leverage as lender of last resort. It can also work together with the Treasury to introduce up-to-date technology in the government securities market, such as a book-entry system to record security ownership and a simultaneous delivery-versus-payment procedure through the central bank's deposit accounts. The monetary authority should ensure that clearing institutions obtain adequate credit lines from banks to act as a backstop in the event of delivery and payment failures.

Conduct of Open Market Operations

Whether it adopts an active or a passive approach, the central bank should start by collecting figures on the supply of and demand for bank reserves. An up-to-date flow of data on bank deposits is particularly important for implementing policy changes sooner rather than later in order to offset undesired trends. In economies undergoing rapid growth or transition, the central bank needs to be especially alert to changes in various measures of the money supply. Even with a passive approach to open market strategy focusing on interest rates, the prompt availability of deposit data will enable the bank to make better projections of the demand for reserves, helping to gauge the effect of open market operations on money market conditions. The central bank will also require estimates of other factors affecting reserve supply, such as government deposits, currency in circulation, foreign exchange, and the float arising from timing differences between crediting and collecting funds in the central bank clearing system. Many of these estimates require close cooperation with the Treasury at a working level.

In practice, the accuracy of reserve estimates needs to judged against incoming evidence on interest rates from the interbank or money market and what that reveals about liquidity pressures. Interpretation of this information should be aided by continuing contacts with the market. Traders from the central bank's open market function should be continually speaking with other traders in an effort to understand the factors influencing market conditions, enabling policymakers to better assess market psychology.

A short-term market rate, in particular an overnight interbank rate (interest charges on funds borrowed to meet the day-to-day residual need for funds in the banking system) may usefully serve as the primary guide for open market operations. Using such a rate does not, however, lessen the need for prompt collection of statistics on basic factors affecting the demand and supply of reserves. An inadequate statistical base would greatly hamper the central bank in its ability to judge whether daily money market rate movements are merely temporary.

Many countries use such day-to-day operating guides as a matter of tactics in pursuing the measures that they use as intermediate policy guides. For example, net domestic assets have been used as an intermediate guide in Poland and Mexico, base money in the Philippines and Brazil, M3 in India and Malaysia, and the foreign exchange rate in Egypt. In many emerging markets, it seems that central banks have generally decided to conduct open market operations on a passive basis, leaving themselves with more flexibility to determine the degree of day-to-day pressure on the banking system and the basic cost of liquidity.

Instruments for Open Market Operations

Without an active secondary market in securities, central banks are in practice limited to open market operations in the primary market. Typically, such operations include auctioning newly issued securities to absorb reserves or auctioning central bank credit to provide reserves. One much used open market operation involves the issue of new Treasury or central bank securities in order to absorb excess liquidity. The Czech Republic and Ghana employ both. Egypt auctions only T-bills to absorb reserves, but also mops up liquidity through the placement of commercial bank deposits directly with the central bank. In the Philippines, however, the use of both T-bill and central bank bills created some confusion and difficulties. In Indonesia, where there is no government debt, the central bank auctions its own bills only to absorb liquidity and purchases bank paper to provide reserves.

If the central bank offers a new Treasury security to absorb reserves, it should be considered as a monetary operation only if the incoming funds are not available to government for spending. The cleanest approach is to set the funds aside in a special account created purely for purposes of monetary policy. Such an account would ensure that bank reserves are reduced "permanently" by the operation, at least until policy is adjusted. In cases where the central bank finds that it overestimated the surplus of reserves, it can buy back the securities before maturity, leaving the special account balance unchanged. Such repurchases before maturity, perhaps followed by subsequent resales as policy is further adjusted, can have the ancillary advantage of helping to develop a secondary market.

Issuing central bank securities should be no more or less costly than offering special Treasury issues created especially for purposes of monetary policy. Choosing between the two types of instruments therefore depends mostly on institutional and market considerations. Central bank issues may be useful, if not necessary, to conduct open market operations in a country, such as Indonesia, where domestic government debt is not allowed. In the Philippines, as noted, the central bank took the same course in the early 1980s because it did not have access to sufficient government debt. Its experience, however, illustrates some of the problems that can occur in a market in which both government and central bank instruments coexist. In particular, the development of an active government securities market appears to have been retarded, rather than stimulated, by large-scale issues of the central bank's own bills. The government thus came to view central bank issues as complicating its policies on interest rates and debt management because they were segmenting what was already a thin market. At the same time, the central bank was taking large losses from operations in foreign exchange and in the restructuring of weak commercial banks, thus putting its credibility into question. By 1993, the central bank was restructured and received a broad portfolio of Treasury securities to facilitate open market operations.

Problems like those in the Philippines may not be inevitable. In Brazil, for instance, where there is a relatively broad overall market, central bank issues have traded well alongside government securities. Open market operations in which special securities are issued for purposes of monetary policy are of most practical use when excess liquidity is flooding the banking system. Because these securities can be bought back before maturity and resold, they can also be employed to adjust to the ebb and flow of liquidity pressure. But they do not provide the same flexibility as open market operations in the secondary market. In the absence of an active money and interbank market, the central bank is deprived of ongoing information about actual and emerging liquidity conditions, which makes planning the timing and size of operations more difficult. The outcome of open market operations may thus be more subject to the vagaries of primary market bidding than to the central bank's prior intentions.

In the absence of an active market for government securities, a special Treasury issue might also be considered as a means of adding to bank reserves needed for long-term growth. This would involve giving the central bank authority to auction a special Treasury deposit that would be created along with the debt issue. Such a special issue, guaranteed by the government, may help strengthen and diversify the central bank's balance sheet.

Flexible Open Market Operations

As their economies expand and their markets mature, more countries are implementing monetary policy through open market operations in the secondary market, mainly in the form of repos and reverse repos. In contrast with outright operations, repos provide temporary financing of reserve shortages and surpluses, but do not directly influence demand and supply in the security that serves as collateral. Most positively, repos tend to enhance liquidity in the underlying securities, helping to develop a more active secondary market. The use of repos with a short maturity should also make it clear to the market that the central bank is encouraging participants to develop as many alternative sources of short-term lending and borrowing as possible.

Repos and reverse repos are ideally suited for offsetting short-term fluctuations that affect bank reserves. They are also useful for offsetting large shifts in liquidity caused, for instance, by a wave of capital inflows or outflows. For these reasons, repos can be expected to become the dominant tool for open market operations, as experience in various countries suggests. Repos can be used in various maturities, although short-term operations tend to dominate. In Brazil, where repos have become the main instrument of policy control, operations are undertaken through informal auctions on a daily basis, with maturities generally overnight. Mexico and Poland also undertake frequent operations with short maturities. Thailand employs an elaborate auction process twice a day, with maturities ranging from overnight out to six months. Maturities appear longest in the Philippines, where reverse repos are used to absorb liquidity, with maturities commonly between one week and one month and with a maximum out to one year.

Outright purchases and sales of Treasury securities in the secondary market are also used in many of these countries. In Brazil they are used to provide or absorb reserves on a more permanent basis. In India and the Philippines, they are considered an important instrument of monetary control and are undertaken on a daily basis. When secondary markets are still comparatively thin, however, outright transactions run a high risk of dominating the market and impeding further development, especially in longer-term sectors.

Government Debt Management

Government decisions on debt management and deposit balances obviously have an impact on the use of open market operations. Sometimes they can help facilitate operations. At other times, they can complicate the task. In all countries, the Treasury and central bank work together on these issues, though with varying degrees of tension and power. On pure debt management decisions, the Treasury in most cases makes the final decision, with the central bank serving as its agent. In areas where governmental operations have a more direct impact on bank reserves, the central bank normally has a bigger say. The particular working relationship differs according to the traditions and financial history of the country.

Whatever the relationship, open market operations will be most effective where the central bank has control over factors that affect the reserve base of the banking system. To help maintain a clear separation between monetary and fiscal policies, it is most desirable if the government debt issued to meet fiscal needs is sold directly into the market by the Treasury, avoiding any potential conflict between debt management and monetary policy needs. Such sales should be in the form of auctions, helping to develop a competitive, deregulated market system. This also avoids pressure on the central bank to facilitate primary market issues at a predetermined rate.

For open market operations, it is particularly important for the central bank to be able to influence, if not control, the Treasury's operating balance with the bank, fluctuations in which affect the supply of bank reserves. It is unusual for the central bank to be given substantial discretionary power over government deposits, but there are exceptions. The Bank of Canada, for instance, has the right to transfer government deposits between itself and commercial banks. Bank Negara Malaysia auctions such deposits as an instrument of policy. Germany's Bundesbank has a veto over the government's ability to hold deposits outside the central bank.

In general, open market operations will function most effectively when the government abides by, and the public believes in, a clear division between debt management and monetary policy operations. In practice, this usually involves an agreement to neutralize the monetary effect of the Treasury's balance or to delegate substantial control over it to the central bank. In virtually all countries, debt management decisions are made with ongoing input from the central bank, both informally and through formal committee structures.

Concluding Observations

There is much to be said for switching to open market operations as soon as possible. Deregulation and globalization of markets make it virtually impossible to use direct controls without adverse side effects. Experience suggests that in practice countries act as if they have little choice except to begin this type of transition. Countries where central banks seem to have lagged often found themselves hampered in meeting policy objectives. On the other hand, availability of market instruments is no guarantee of success, as recent experience in Mexico shows. Clearly, an arsenal of open market instruments is a necessary condition for success, but not a sufficient one.

Most countries have begun making complementary adjustments in reserve requirements consistent with the growing importance of open market operations. They have also been restricting access to the discount window, which has nevertheless remained open as a safety valve. Still, for most emerging markets and transitional economies, which are prone to surges in liquidity and sudden capital flows and with markets at varying stages of development, a complementary mix of all monetary instruments may be the best solution. Transformation of markets usually occurs in two stages: the establishment of a primary market followed by development of a secondary market. The initial transition is much easier to accomplish. Well-functioning secondary markets, however, must develop largely within the private sector, although the central bank can exert some influence through the legal, regulatory, and payments infrastructure. It is difficult for the central bank to accelerate development through transactions alone, as this risks dominating the market. Repos and reverse repos would appear to be the most effective instruments for encouraging such development. It is crucial, however, to develop an interbank market, which can then provide signals for policy. There are risks if the central bank relies excessively on operations in private paper, which can become illiquid. In the absence of an active government securities market, the use of the central bank's own issues, or of special Treasury issues designated for monetary policy purposes, might be considered as a supplement.